100

THINGS TO DO IN
LITTLE ROCK
BEFORE YOU
DIE

100

THINGS TO DO IN
LITTLE ROCK
BEFORE YOU
DIE

Juliana, Thanks for the support o God Bless.

CELIA ANDERSON

REEDY PRESS

Library of Congress Control Number: 2016937273

ISBN: 9781681060422

Design by Jill Halpin

Cover photo courtesy of the Little Rock Convention & Visitors Bureau.

Printed in the United States of America
16 17 18 19 20   5 4 3 2 1

Please note that websites, phone numbers, addresses, and company names are subject to change or cancellation. We did our best to relay the most accurate information available, but due to circumstances beyond our control, please do not hold us liable for misinformation. When exploring new destinations, please do your homework before you go.

DEDICATION

To the city of Little Rock, thank you for giving me wings.

• •

CONTENTS

• •

Music and Entertainment

Sports and Recreation

• •

Culture and History

• •

Shopping and Fashion

• •

PREFACE

So you've never been to Little Rock, eh? It's okay. We like to keep the place a secret, this way we can have all the fun to ourselves! Arkansas's capital city is certainly a pleasant surprise. I'm sure you've heard that we are home to the Clinton Presidential Library and the Little Rock Nine, but did you know that Forbes Travel Guide named Little Rock one of America's Five Secret Foodie Cities? And for good reason. You will find out why in the food and drink section!

One thing that adds most to this city's vitality is the people. Southern hospitality is real in Little Rock. Whether it's holding the door or giving a friendly wave to a passing stranger, courtesy is engraved in our DNA. Little Rock is also located in the center of the country, which makes the city an easy drive from several major metropolises. Unlike any other midsize city, Little Rock has no concept of size. With a population of almost two hundred thousand, we have a big city attitude. Separated into several different neighborhoods, each part of Little Rock has its own style complete with unique ways of expressing them.

I was raised in fun-loving midtown, and now reside in family-centered West Little Rock with my only daughter, Gabrielle. For many years, in between those two locations, I lived abroad and in several major cities, constantly searching for a place to call home. After fifteen years, I realized that Little Rock was that place. I bring you *100 Things to Do in Little Rock Before You Die* in an effort to share my home with you. Come eat at our restaurants, explore our history, but most of all, enjoy our hospitality.

Of course there are more than one hundred things to do in Little Rock, but this book will get you started on your journey to experiencing the magic of the capital city. Take a stroll across the Big Dam Bridge or wander into The Heights neighborhood. Whatever you decide, be careful, you may want to call Little Rock home as well.

—Celia Anderson

Photos provided courtesy of
the Little Rock Convention & Visitors Bureau

ACKNOWLEDGMENTS

This girl first acknowledges God for his many blessings.

Reedy Press, you have been amazing. Thank you for choosing me to share my city with the world. I would also like to thank Dorothy Hall, Gretchen Hall, and Alan Sims for bringing me home to do a job that I love. Life is indeed better with a southern accent! To all the local business owners who help make Little Rock one astonishing city, I am grateful for your hard work.

To my mother Sarah Hinton, sister Latonia Wimberly, daughter Gabrielle Anderson, and my very best friend Addis Huyler—thank you all for being my rocks. My uncle Willie Hinton, who is single-handedly responsible for our family settling in Arkansas, I thank God every day for your wisdom—I am who I am because of you. Finally, to Bruce Moore, Little Rock's city manager, your love for Little Rock is contagious, and our city is better because of you. Thank you for your service.

Photos provided courtesy of
the Little Rock Convention & Visitors Bureau.

FOOD AND DRINK

DRINK LIKE A LOCAL
WITH LOCALLY LABELED

In Little Rock we like to keep things local, even our alcohol. With several homegrown craft breweries, wineries, and a distillery, we have a drink for everyone. Locally Labeled is your passport to the local drinking scene. The concept is simple: first you visit the Locally Labeled website below, then download the passport, visit participating locations, and get customized stickers to win a Locally Labeled t-shirt or coaster! Locally Labeled is a must do for anyone visiting the city. You will experience Arkansas's first distillery, Rock Town Distillery, founded by Phil Brandon in 2010. Here you can find a Hot Doctor and Apple Pie, both over ice and in a glass! Then there is Diamond Bear Brewery, which is home to their famous strawberry blonde beer. Whether your drink of choice is beer, wine or whiskey, Little Rock has a spot for you!

Locally Labeled
www.littlerock.com/things-to-do/locallylabeled.aspx

TIP
Don't want to drive? No problem, find 23 friends and take the Toddy Trolley!
www.toddytrolley.com
501-603-0113

Locally Labeled Participants

Blue Canoe Brew Co.
425 E. Third St., Little Rock
501-492-9378
www.bluecanoebrewco.com

Damgoode Pies Brewpub
500 President Clinton Ave.
Little Rock
501-353-1724
www.damgoodepies.com

Diamond Bear Brewing Co.
600 N. Broadway St.
North Little Rock
501-708-2337
www.diamondbear.com

Lost Forty Brewing
501 Byrd St., Little Rock
501-319-7275
www.lost40brewing.com

Refined Ale Brewery
2221 S. Cedar St., Little Rock
501-663-9901

Stone's Throw Brewing
402 E. Ninth St., Little Rock
501-244-9154
www.stonesthrowbeer.com

Vino's Brewpub
923 W. Seventh St., Little
Rock
501-375-8466
www.vinosbrewpub.com

**An Enchanting Evening
Winery**
29300 AR-300, Roland
anenchantingevening.com

**River Bottom Winery at
BoBrook Farms**
13810 Combee La., Roland
501-868-8860, 501-519-5666
bobrookfarms.com

Rock Town Distillery
1216 E. Sixth St., Little Rock
501-907-5244
www.rocktowndistillery.com

START
AT THE BEGINNING AT FRANKE'S

What better place to start your Little Rock food journey, than at the beginning? That's right, Franke's Cafeteria is Arkansas's oldest restaurant. Dating back to 1919, this family-owned business has survived in Arkansas for nearly a century. The original vision of C.A. Franke was a doughnut shop opened in 1919, and by 1924 Franke's Cafeteria was born. W.J. Franke was the second generation to run the cafeteria before passing it on to W.K. "Bill" Franke in 1983. Today Bill and his wife Carolyn still run the business and daughter Christen has joined the ranks as the manager of "Sack It" by Franke's, where they specialize in to-go orders. Franke's now has three locations in Little Rock, all serving up award-winning southern home cooking. Visit Franke's, where you are certain to feel at home!

Franke's Market Place
Market Place Shopping Center
11121 N. Rodney Parham Rd.,
Little Rock
501-225-4487
frankescafeteria.com

Franke's Downtown
Regions Center Building
400 Broadway St., Little Rock
501-372-1919

"Sack It" by Franke's
Regions Center Building
400 Broadway St., Little Rock
501-372-4177

EAT LIKE A PRESIDENT
AT DOE'S EAT PLACE

Looking for a dive with food that tastes like your mother's? Doe's Eat Place is the place to be. You won't find fancy tablecloths or waiters and waitresses dressed in their Sunday best, but you will find steaks that put any world-class steakhouse to shame. It all began when George Eldridge grew tired of flying friends and clients to Doe's Eat Place in Greenville, Mississippi, where he found the best tamales and steaks around. Soon he contracted the right to bring both the name and menu to Little Rock. Not only did it save him a lot of gas, it quickly became a local favorite. Doe's most famous regular is none other than former President Bill Clinton. In 1992, when then-candidate Clinton was interviewed by *Rolling Stone* magazine, the backdrop was none other than Doe's Eat Place.

1023 W. Markham St., Little Rock
501-376-1195
www.doeseatplace.net

ENJOY UPSCALE CUISINE
AT THE CAPITAL HOTEL

There is no place in Little Rock like the Capital Hotel. The boutique property has been the very definition of class in the city for over thirty years. Aside from offering a unique hotel experience, the Capital Hotel also serves up exquisite cuisine. They have two restaurants on property, One Eleven and the Capital Bar and Grill. One Eleven is the total dining experience complete with upscale cuisine, excellent service, and a very inviting atmosphere. There you can enjoy the food of award-winning Chef Joel Antunes. The Capital Bar and Grill is where you go for drinks and comfort food. The popular bar is perfect for after-work cocktails and catching some jazz from the Ted Ludwig Trio who plays there every Thursday-Sunday.

111 W. Markham St., Little Rock
501-374-7474
www.capitalhotel.com

TIP
The Capital Hotel is famous for their roasted pecans and pimento cheese. Try them both.

HANG WITH WAYNE
AT CHICKEN WANG'S CAFÉ

It all started at a local bar where Little Rock professionals spent their happy hours. Wayne Fuller, a young aspiring restaurant owner, signed on to keep their bellies full of his original lemon pepper chicken wings. It did not take long for Wayne to gain the nickname Chicken Wang, and now fifteen years later, that name graces the fronts of two restaurants. Tucked away in the inner city, both locations have a charming interior, with warm southern hospitality. The menu includes all flavors from lemon pepper to barbecue. You can sit in and catch up on sports or call your order in for pickup. Whichever you choose, you'll never have another wing—Wang's will be all you desire.

8320 Colonel Glenn Rd., Little Rock
501-562-1303

HAVE A STEAK
AT ARTHUR'S PRIME STEAKHOUSE

Thinking of proposing to the love of your life? Arthur's is the place to do it. You can tuck away in the private wine cellar, which creates an atmosphere fit for royalty. While you are there, enjoy a bottle of wine from either wine vault. The first holds premium American, Italian, Chilean, and Australian wines, and the second houses strictly French and older vintage wines. If the cellar is not available, try the Crystal or Mark's rooms, which also offer private dining. Whether you choose to dine privately or not, one thing is promised: you will experience grades of beef ranging from dry aged prime natural to the Australian Wagyu and the Japanese KOBE. Arthur's has quickly climbed the ladder of steakhouse fame. You won't be disappointed.

27 Rahling Cir., Suite A-1, Little Rock
501-821-1838
www.arthursprimesteakhouse.com

TIP
Not feeling steak? No worries, Oceans at Arthur's is top-of-the-line seafood, and it is right next door.

While we are talking beef, try these local favorite burger joints!

David's Burgers
3510 Landers Road, North Little Rock
501-353-0387
www.davidsburgers.com

101 South Bowman Road, Little Rock
501-227-8333

Park Plaza Mall (Food Court), Little Rock
501-603-5151

Ottenheimer Market Hall
400 President Clinton Ave., Little Rock

Monkey Burger
4424 Frazier Pike, Little Rock
501-490-2222

Big Orange
207 N. University Ave Ste. 100, Little Rock
501-379-8715
www.bigorangeburger.com

17809 Chenal Pkwy, STE.G-101, Little Rock
501-821-1515

CREATE A MEMORY
AT CACHE

In the heart of downtown Little Rock, Cache has quickly become a local favorite. The city can thank Rush and Payne Harding for their vision of culinary greatness. The father-son duo wanted to bring a contemporary dining experience to downtown, one that fostered the spirit of togetherness. It is not uncommon for business men and women to find themselves at Cache winding down from the busy work day. The upstairs bar and balcony that overlooks President Clinton Avenue offers a place to relax, enjoy signature cocktails, and listen to live music. Cache also offers a banquet room for private events and has become a go-to for corporate meetings and events. Dining at Cache will be an experience that you won't soon forget. What are you waiting for? Create a memory at Cache!

425 President Clinton Ave., Little Rock
501-850-0265
www.cachelittlerock.com

DINE WITH THE BEST
AT SONNY WILLIAMS' STEAK ROOM

Be sure to dress to impress and make a reservation if you plan on going to Sonny Williams'. Thrillist.com named the downtown steak room Arkansas's best steakhouse. Since Little Rock is home to many, this is no small feat! Located in the River Market District downtown, Sonny Williams' opened in Little Rock in 1999. Since then they have served a steak that is both aged and tender. Pair it with a wine from an extensive wine list and delicious sides of your choice. For non-beef eaters, the finest pork, lamb, chicken, and seafood are also on the menu. With complimentary valet and stellar service, Sonny Williams' has overlooked no detail. Did I mention they also have a piano bar?

500 President Clinton Ave., Suite 100, Little Rock
501-324-2999
www.sonnywilliamssteakroom.com

CELEBRATE SOUTHERN CULTURE
AT SOUTH ON MAIN

Chef Matthew Bell is Little Rock's most creative chef, with a unique flair for culinary cuisine. The lunch menu at South on Main includes tasty entrées like Bologna and Egg Sandwich with BBQ Sauce, Chow Chow and a Fried Egg on Texas Toast. If you can wait until dinner, you can have Duck Breast with Nellie Mae's Cornbread Dressing, Granny Beans & Giblet Gravy. There are also mouthwatering vegetarian options, such as Hoppin' John Veggie Burger: Black Eyed Pea & Rice Patty with Pickled Jalapeño, Onion, Spring Greens, Crystal Mayo & Fries. While you are dining, you can also enjoy programming directly from *Oxford American* magazine, including film screenings and musical performances. South on Main is more than a restaurant, it's a community movement, the heartbeat of SoMa, Little Rock's Southside Main Street project.

1304 Main St., Little Rock
501-244-9600
southonmain.com

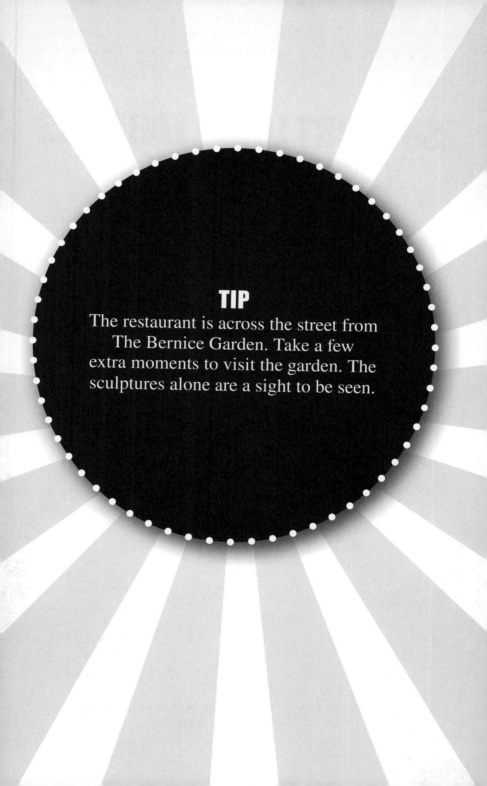

TIP

The restaurant is across the street from The Bernice Garden. Take a few extra moments to visit the garden. The sculptures alone are a sight to be seen.

SUPPORT LOCAL FARMERS
AT THE ROOT CAFE

Since 2008, The Root has been an avid supporter of Arkansas farmers. Their mission is to build community through local food. Because of this, they have become much more than a restaurant. Located in the heart of the South on Main (SoMa) neighborhood, The Root has lived up to its name by creating a sound foundation on which the community can grow. Aside from great food, they offer several different activities from workshops to beard-growing contests! It is not uncommon to see people sitting along the sidewalk dining area conversing about environmental issues. The Root Cafe is a favorite among clean eaters. A few of the farmers they support include Apple Jack Farm in North Little Rock, Armstead Mountain Farm in Jerusalem, Little Rock Urban Farming in Little Rock, and Pulaski Heights Elementary Garden in Little Rock.

1500 Main St., Little Rock
501-414-0423
www.therootcafe.com

TASTE BRAZILIAN CUISINE
AT CAFÉ BOSSA NOVA

Thanks to native Brazilian Rosalia Monroe and her family for bringing Brazil to Little Rock. Enjoy authentic Brazilian food in a culturally astute atmosphere. Menu items include starters like Pão De Queijo, a Brazilian-style cheese bread made with gluten free yucca root flour, milk, eggs, and cheese. Or try a main course such as Panquecas De Frango Brazilian chicken crepes, baked in Catupiry cheese sauce, or homemade marinara sauce served over rice and a Mista salad. As you can see, there is nothing American about Bossa Nova. For dessert, you can slide next door to Rosalia's Bakery for more traditional treats. Oh, don't forget Sunday brunch from 10:30 a.m. to 2 p.m., where you can enjoy live music and cuisine. But get there early, it's a local after-church favorite.

2701 Kavanaugh Blvd., Little Rock
501-614-6682
www.cafebossanova.com

BE BRAVE. BE NEW.
AT BRAVE NEW RESTAURANT

The awards for this restaurant go on and on. From best romantic restaurant to best chef to best business lunch, Brave New Restaurant has won them all. Service here is second to none. The staff is friendly and knowledgeable and the food is impeccable. Situated on the Arkansas River, you can choose to dine inside or outside for a scenic view. Either way, it will be money well spent. When driving there, be careful not to miss it. It is on the second floor of an office building, so you have to take the elevator up. Once you get there the ride will have been worth it. Offering a classy atmosphere, with oil lamp candles on the tables and a menu with something for everyone, Brave New has taken its spot among the restaurant elite. Going for lunch? May I recommend the Nontraditional Grilled Cheese? Trust me on this one.

2300 Cottondale La., Suite 105, Little Rock
501-663-2677
www.bravenewrestaurant.com

LOVE THE FOOD
AT CAFE PREGO

Three words describe this restaurant: great Italian food. Prego takes pride in every dish on their one-page menu. This is not your typical stuffy place with wait staff running around in neckties. No, Prego is down-home Italian. The small locally-owned place has no interest in keeping up with the Jones's, only serving immaculate entrées. This they do very well. The focaccia bread is always a great start. Many recommend the Tortellini Carbonara; it has quite the reputation around town. If you are the type of diner who does not need bells and whistles, Prego is the place for you. The charming establishment has only one thing in mind, serving up good food. If weather permits, ask to sit on the patio. You'll be glad you did.

5510 Kavanaugh Blvd., Little Rock
501-663-5355

GRATIFY YOUR SWEET TOOTH
AT CUPCAKES ON KAVANAUGH

Owner Christy Milligan is from a long line of extraordinary bakers and the tradition continues through her. Her love for the art can be felt when you walk through the door as she left no detail to the imagination. A small charming space, her shop is decorated with the same love that goes into every cupcake that goes out of the door. Matching the quality baking that both her mother and grandmother believed in, is what Christy is all about. She even got her husband Chris in on all the fun! A combination of both old and new, whether its classic vanilla or razorback red velvet specialty flavors will keep you coming back for more. They also cater, so if you want to add a dash of style and a pinch of brilliance to any event, Cupcakes on Kavanaugh is the way to go. You can taste the love in every bite.

5625 Kavanaugh Blvd., Little Rock
501-664-CAKE (2253)
http://www.eatacupcake.com/

**What are pastries without coffee?
Try these local coffee shops**

Mylo Coffee
2715 Kavanaugh Blvd., Little Rock
501-747-1880
www.mylocoffee.com

Guillermo's Gourmet Coffee
10700 N. Rodney Parham Rd., Suite A2, Little Rock
501-228-4448

River City Coffee
2913 Kavanaugh Blvd., Little Rock
501-661-1496
www.rivercitycoffeelr.com

Sufficient Grounds Café
124 W. Capitol Ave., Little Rock
501-372-1009
www.sufficientgroundscafe.com

Mugs Cafe
515 Main St., North Little Rock
501-379-9109
www.mugscafe.org

Andina Cafe
433 E. Third St., Little Rock
501-376-2326
andina-cafe.com

DON'T DANCE
AT SAMANTHA'S TAP ROOM
AND WOOD GRILL

At first glance you may mistake this for a dance studio, but please do not be confused. There is no tap dancing around anything at Samantha's Tap Room, they are straight upscale and comfortable with astounding fare. Located in one of Little Rock's newest districts, The Main Street Creative Corridor, Samantha's has been instrumental in breathing life back into Main Street. Offering their entire beer and wine list on tap (thirty-two beers and twenty wines) makes them not only a popular spot, but also the only restaurant in Arkansas to do so. Winner of the 2015 Free Flow Wine Keggy People's Choice Award, Samantha's has received national recognition, and rightfully so. The menu selection is just as broad as the wine and beer list, and it's all cooked by way of wood fire.

322 S. Main St., Little Rock
501-379-8019
www.samstap.com

STUFF YOURSELF
AT FLYING FISH

No, the fish do not fly, but they do fry and they never disappoint! Flying Fish is "fast-casual"-style dining. You line up, order, pick your seat, and wait for your number to be called. While you wait, enjoy fresh hushpuppies and coleslaw, but save room for your entrée. If you like East Texas fish joints, you will love Flying Fish. Here you can get shrimp, oysters, crab legs, and crawfish in season. There is also a special selection of trout, grilled salmon, or tilapia presented daily. For the non-seafood lovers, they have fresh salads, hamburgers, and chicken tenders. The best thing is, Flying Fish is open seven days a week from 11 a.m. to 10 p.m. So whatever time you ride into town, stop at Flying Fish. You will be glad you did.

511 President Clinton Ave., Little Rock
501-375-3474
www.flyingfishinthe.net

SOAK YOUR BREAD
AT SIM'S BAR-B-QUE

Have you ever been to a place where the sauce is so good, you just want to soak your bread in it? Sim's vinegar mustard brown sugar sauce is just that good. Started in 1937, Sim's Bar-B-Que is one of the very few black-owned businesses that survived integration. The original location on thirty-third Street was the lunch time favorite for people from all walks of life. Today Sim's has several sites throughout the city and even offers catering. Mr. Settlers owns the Broadway restaurant and is responsible for the incorporation of the business. At the Broadway location you will find the same crowd that frequented the original restaurant, plus a few new faces. Known for their spare ribs and pork or beef sandwiches, Sim's is the place to go when you want good barbecue with a flavor unique only to Little Rock.

2415 S. Broadway St., Little Rock
501-372-6868

1307 John Barrow Rd., Little Rock
501-224-2057

7601 Geyer Springs Rd., Little Rock
501-562-8844

www.simsbbqar.com

SIT ON THE DECK
AT CAJUN'S WHARF

If the weather is right, you want to sit on the deck. Trust me. It's like being on top of the world! Cajun's Wharf has it all: a three-level bar area with plenty of seating, good food, live music, and a stellar reputation. Here you can enjoy seafood or aged Angus beef, wine, or a mixed cocktail, a late night party band or an early evening dinner. The choice is yours. Located behind the commercial warehouses along the waterfront, Cajun's also has great views of the Arkansas River. Check out their website to see what band is playing. Who knows? It may be a band you like. If not, the atmosphere will be so good that you won't notice the music!

2400 Cantrell Rd., Little Rock
501-375-5351
www.cajunswharf.com

GO
TO SO

Ever had a fried green tomato crab cake? No? What are you waiting for? Go to SO! This intimate restaurant will have you bragging to your friends. The mellow ambiance is sure to relax your spirit. Tucked away between two of Little Rock's best neighborhoods, The Heights and Hillcrest, SO is the perfect blend of class and sophistication. When you get there, say hi to Theo, longtime bartender who remembers everyone by name. Be sure to call for a reservation, as a table can be hard to come by. SO is well known for its food and service. In fact, the Sea Bass has never had a complaint! There is also a private lounge downstairs from the main dining room that can accommodate larger groups. Did I mention SO has a patio? And you never have to worry about the weather. SO has the capability to cover it completely if need be.

3610 Kavanaugh Blvd., Little Rock
501-663-1464
www.sorestaurantbar.com

FIND MOLE
AT FONDA MEXICAN CUISINE AND TEQUILA BAR

A wise man from El Paso once told me, "If a Mexican restaurant does not have mole on the menu, it is not Mexican!" He was serious. Whether he is right or not is up to you, but Fonda has mole on the menu AND it tastes good. Everything about this restaurant is authentic Mexican from the music to the décor and certainly the cuisine. Margaritas are made fresh and the selection of appetizers is impressive with pezcadillas, chicken flautas, and chile poblano cheese quesadillas with guacamole all on the menu. Fonda also offers Sunday brunch and catering for special events. Although there is no official website, you can visit Fonda on Facebook. Fonda is the restaurant where authenticity is a habit.

400 N. Bowman Rd., Little Rock
501-313-4120

DRINK WINE
AT ZIN URBAN WINE AND BEER BAR

Open seven days a week and with over thirty-eight wines served by the glass, Zin is the place to be for wine connoisseurs. Their premium selection includes brands from all around the world. The quaint space makes it perfect for intimate conversation or a night out with friends. If you need something to accompany your beverage, the tapas menu offers a variety of options from gourmet nuts to stuffed bell peppers. For non-wine-drinkers, Zin also has an assortment of premium beers that are sure to satisfy. Don't forget to call for a reservation; Zin fills up quickly. You also want to check to see if they have live music. Every once in a while you can catch a great local artist blessing the mic.

300 River Market Ave., Little Rock
501-246-4786
www.zinlr.com

TAKE YOUR PICK
AT THE RIVER MARKET'S
OTTENHEIMER MARKET HALL

With room for fifteen vendors, the River Market has an option for even the pickiest eater. Here you won't find fast food chains, but a bazaar of food including Sweet Soul Southern Café, Big on Tokyo, Rivershore Eatery, Jay's Pizza, and The Veg, which brands itself as Little Rock's premier place for vegetarians. Once you have decided what to eat, you can sit in the large seating area and log onto free Wi-Fi. The hall opens at 7 a.m., which makes it a good choice for breakfast, and does not close until 7 p.m. When you are done eating, pop into Shop the Rock and pick up some Little Rock souvenirs that will remind you of your trip for years to come.

400 President Clinton Ave., Little Rock
501-376-4781
www.rivermarket.info/eat

TIP
If you like choices, slide over to The Food Truck Stop at Station 801. There is inside seating and something new every day!
Open Mon.-Fri. 11:00-2:30

801 Chester St., Little Rock
www.lrstation801.com

CREATE A SALAD
AT ZAZA'S FINE SALAD AND WOOD OVEN PIZZA

With several home-grown ingredients to choose from, ZAZA's is farm-to-table in true form. Create your own salad with your favorite toppings or simply pick one from the menu. Located in The Heights District in Little Rock, ZAZA's is known for having one of the best salads in town. If you are looking for more than a salad, the wood oven pizza is made fresh with a few ingredients that ZAZA's takes pride in. According to their website, they are FANATICAL about certified San Marzano tomatoes and Molino Caputo Tipo 00, a true Italian doppio zero wheat flour. Want to know if those ingredients make a difference? Dare to be creative-—pop into ZAZA's for a salad and pizza. For dessert, enjoy a serving of gelato, made fresh each morning.

5600 Kavanaugh Blvd., Suite 100, Little Rock
501-661-9292
www.zazapizzaandsalad.com

GET COMFORTABLE
AT CRUSH WINE BAR

Wine bars are normally places where people sit around with their pinkies in the air, swirling glasses and tossing around words like balance, length and finish. While there are some connoisseurs on staff and as loyal customers, don't expect stuffy—Crush doesn't do stuffy. They do inviting and comfortable with an unpretentious classy twist. With both classic and trendy brands, there is a wine on the menu for everyone. Happy hour is from 4 p.m. to 7 p.m., when you can get great deals. Crush is located in the Argenta District of North Little Rock. Oh, I almost forgot, just in case you don't drink wine, they also serve beer.

318 Main St., North Little Rock
501-374-9463

TIP
Hang around the Argenta Arts District for a while.
It's full of life and local flavor.
www.argentaartsdistrict.org

DINE
AT FORTY TWO

Wondering why it's called Forty Two? You guessed it! Arkansas is the birthplace of the forty-second president of the United States. A full-service restaurant, with simple but classy décor inside the William J. Clinton Presidential Library, Forty Two offers a variety of modern menu items and service fit for a president. It's the perfect backdrop for a business lunch or to catch up with an old friend. The most surprising thing about Forty Two is the prices. Not only is the food good, it's reasonable. If you are in town on a weekend, have Sunday brunch there. You will be glad you did. The old adage, "you get what you pay for", does not apply to Forty Two. Here you certainly get more.

1200 President Clinton Ave., Little Rock
501-537-0042
www.dineatfortytwo.com

EXPERIENCE ITALY
AT BRUNO'S LITTLE ITALY

Founded in Little Rock in 1949, Bruno's Little Italy has been serving authentic Neapolitan entrées for over fifty years. The restaurant has grown from its humble beginnings to a premier location in the heart of downtown. They were one of the first facilities to sign on to assist with the revitalization of Main Street, but it did not take others long to follow. It is this commitment to community that makes Bruno's a mainstay on the national culinary scene. A winner of several awards, including the Great Gold Cup Trophy of Honor for the best Italian food in the United States by Fair of Rome (tied with Mama Leone's in New York City), the Bruno family has succeeded in bringing a small piece of Italy to Arkansas.

310 S. Main St., Little Rock
501-372-7866
www.brunoslittleitaly.com

FEEL GOOD
AT THE MAIN CHEESE

The Main Cheese has something for the whole family, but the main thing is the grilled cheese! Served on potato bread with your choice of fries, chips, or coleslaw, it is filling and delicious. If you want a healthier choice, there is a smoothie menu and you can pick your own mix of ingredients. This locally-owned restaurant specializes in high-quality food. The Main Cheese came from humble beginnings to meaningful vision and translated both into extraordinary food. Customers could not agree more. The farmer's chopped salad with salmon and skirt steak on ciabatta are a few favorites. Whatever your palate, there is something on the menu at the Main Cheese and if you can't decide, go with the main thing!

14524 Cantrell Rd., Little Rock
501-367-8082

FALL IN LOVE WITH SUSHI
AT KEMURI

Master Chef Greg Wallis has given Little Rock a taste of Tokyo. Kemuri has added something to the Little Rock food scene that is new and fresh. The self-proclaimed "best sushi in town" can be found here. Locals rave about the Crazy Monkey Roll, but traditional rolls are also available. If you are not a sushi lover, Kemuri doubles as a full-scale restaurant with traditional Japanese-style grilling. The Panang Curry will leave you raving. Located in one of Little Rock's most eclectic upscale neighborhoods, Kemuri shares the strip with several other local businesses. After dinner you can walk down the sidewalk for drinks Next Bistro and Bar.

2601 Kavanaugh Blvd., Little Rock
501-660-4100
www.kemurirestaurant.com

ENJOY SATURDAY BRUNCH
AT RED DOOR

Red Door's patio is the place to be for Saturday brunch. Sometimes the wait is over an hour for the southern cuisine. What's so special about Red Door? It's the chef. Chef Mark Abernathy is a mainstay on the Little Rock food scene. He has been the face of many popular restaurants and now adds Red Door to his résumé. While most chefs view the kitchen as their workplace, Mark is different. He is active in the community and passionate about passing the art of cooking on to the next generation. He takes his skill into the world and tries to make a difference. You can taste his passion through his food at Red Door. Hint: If the line is long at Red Door, go next door to Loca Luna. Chef Abernathy is the mastermind behind it too.

3701 Old Cantrell Rd., Little Rock
501-666-8482
www.reddoorrestaurant.net

COOL OFF
AT LE POPS

Gone are the days when Popsicles were just Kool-Aid on a stick. Le Pops has transformed that simple concept into Popsicle heaven. Each treat is handmade with the best ingredients. Le Pops's bold and unusual flavors set them apart. Ever had Strawberry and Basil? Yeah, neither have I, but it's on the menu! They also serve vegan and non-dairy—this way everyone can enjoy a tasty treat. For those cold days, Le Pops even has Hot Pops. Imagine a chilled raspberry pop placed in a hot coffee, or a salted caramel pop soaked in hot chocolate. Le Pops has a variety of options. It's the perfect place for moms who are looking for healthy ice cream alternatives for themselves or their children.

5501 Kavanaugh Blvd., Little Rock
501-313-9558
www.lepops.com

SIT AROUND THE DINNER TABLE
AT CIAO BACI

Ciao Baci feels like home. What was once a nice bungalow in the Hillcrest neighborhood is now a comfortable restaurant. Complete with a porch swing, the atmosphere couldn't be more inviting. Specializing in service, Ciao Baci's goal is to make you feel like you are sharing a holiday meal with family. Don't let the name fool you, though, it is not an Italian restaurant. With a Mediterranean-inspired menu, there is a variety of interesting and innovative options from which to choose. The calamari and house sangria are their specialties. Enjoy either on the patio or the inside dining room. If you just want to stop in for a drink, happy hour is always happening—Ciao Baci is known for their drink specials.

605 Beechwood St., Little Rock
501-603-0238
www.ciaobaci.org

RELIVE YOUR TEENAGE YEARS
AT PIZZA CAFE

Locals have kept this place in business for over twenty years. We love it. So much that servers know you by name and can deliver your order without even asking. I am convinced that if we still had sock hops, Pizza Cafe would be where teenagers would meet before and after. In fact, now forty-year-olds will sit around the establishment telling stories of their high school days at Pizza Cafe. It is the hole in the wall that sucks you in, and you keep coming back for more. More friendly service, more cold beer, and more pizza. All are welcomed at either location. The original location is on Rebsamen Park Road; those walls hold great memories of Arkansans from all walks of life.

1517 Rebsamen Park Rd., Little Rock
501-664-6133

14710 Cantrell Rd., Little Rock
501-868-2600

www.pizzacafelr.com

SATISFY YOUR SOUL
AT KITCHEN EXPRESS

Kitchen Express is soul food heaven. Serving up homemade rolls, smoked turkey legs, fried chicken, and barbecued ribs, this cafeteria-style restaurant is Little Rock's go-to for soul food. Lunch time at Kitchen Express is always busy. The love for the food and fast service brings together people from all walks of life. However, you don't want to miss out on the country-style breakfast. Where else can you get biscuits and gravy and smothered potatoes at the drive-through? Kitchen Express also caters and has a banquet room for those who have large numbers to feed.

4600 Asher Ave., Little Rock
501-663-3500
www.thekitchenexpress.com

After you eat, enjoy urban adult nightlife nearby!

La'Changes
3325 W. Roosevelt Rd., Little Rock
501-661-9810

Trois
4314 Asher Ave., Little Rock
501-663-7800
www.troisnightclub.com

Jazzi's
5200 Asher Ave., Little Rock
501-562-6919

Club Envy
7200 Colonel Glenn Rd., Little Rock
501-569-9113

Photos provided courtesy of
the Little Rock Convention & Visitors Bureau.

CHAT WITH A FRIEND
AT COMMUNITY BAKERY

The name says it all. This is the community's bakery. The place for the people. And it has been since 1947. I'm convinced that some major business deals have been signed within these four walls. Community Bakery is where both business professionals and artists meet. Thanks to Ralph Hinson, the company's founder, for his vision. Although the first location was in North Little Rock, it moved to the capital city in 1952. Today, it's owned by Joe Fox and while it has two Little Rock locations, the Main Street bakery remains the heart of the business. Community Bakery is where Arkansans go to chat with friends!

1200 Main St., Little Rock
501-375-6418

270 S. Shackleford Rd., Little Rock
501-224-1656

www.communitybakery.com

ARKANSAS ARTS CENTER

CARRIE REMMEL DICKINSON FOUNTAIN

MUSIC AND ENTERTAINMENT

GET FESTIVE
AT RIVERFEST

For well over thirty years Arkansans have come from all over the state for Riverfest. I have memories from grade school of me and family heading downtown to the riverfront for good food and fun! Now this is the place to go for live music. Past lineups include Willie Nelson, Blue October, Hootie and the Blowfish, and then just Hootie (Darius Rucker) by himself. Readers who love hip-hop and R & B will be interested to learn that Ruben Studdard, Snoop Dogg, Macy Gray, Boyz II Men, and Arrested Development have all performed at Riverfest. The great thing about Riverfest is that no matter your taste, there will be a concert for you! Go to their website. Riverfest is a Little Rock experience you don't want to miss!

www.riverfestarkansas.com

TIP
Riverfest always concludes with a fireworks show, a great family event. All you need is a blanket or lawn chairs!

SPEND A DAY
AT THE ARKANSAS STATE FAIR

If you are looking for fun for the whole family or just an adult outing, in October of every year, the Arkansas State Fair has it all. This is not some fly by night carnival with impossible to win games, this is the real deal. Complete with livestock shows, pageants, and concerts there is something for everyone. If you are looking for southern fried desserts, look no further. They fry anything from Oreos to Twinkes! You can also enjoy a turkey leg or a foot-long corndog, both made with special down south love. Aside from entertainment and southern fried cuisine, The Arkansas State Fair is also committed to providing educational opportunities. Thanks to the Arkansas Livestock Association, an organization committed to youth development, here you can learn about agriculture, livestock and technology. The Arkansas state Fair makes Little Rock the place to be in October!

2600 Howard Street, Little Rock
501-372-8341
http://www.arkansasstatefair.com/

LAUGH
AT THE LOONY BIN COMEDY CLUB

Little Rock is certainly delighted to be one of only four cities where the Loony Bin Comedy Club brings laughter. (The other locations are Wichita, Tulsa, and Oklahoma City.) Sometimes you need a break from the bar scene and movie theaters, and Loony Bin provides the city with a funny alternative. It is not uncommon to catch some great up-and-coming comedians as well as the legends. You can also enjoy dinner or appetizers while you laugh. Loony Bin is perfect for date night or hanging with friends. Either way you are sure to laugh until your stomach hurts! Check their website or call for show times and to find out which comedian is on the bill. You can pay at the door, but I don't recommend it as this place is always sold out!

10301 N. Rodney Parham Rd., Little Rock
501-228-5555
www.loonybincomedy.com

CATCH A PERFORMANCE
AT THE ROBINSON PERFORMANCE HALL

This historic performance hall has served as the place in Little Rock for all things music, dance, and theater since 1937. Robinson has been home to many greats including Elvis Presley, Ella Fitzgerald, Gene Autry, Glenn Campbell, and Nat King Cole. With a grand re-opening scheduled for November 2016 after a nearly $70 million renovation, Little Rock's landmark facility will return better than ever. Enjoy the orchestra, ballet, or a theatrical production of your choice. For the first time, *Phantom of the Opera* is on the bill for 2017, and this is just the beginning. With the expansions and upgrades, look for booking agency Celebrity Attractions to have many more Broadway productions take interest. Just in case you are looking for a place to host a meeting, Robinson is connected to the DoubleTree hotel and will feature a fabulous ballroom overlooking the river.

426 W. Markham St., Little Rock
501-376-4781
www.robinsoncentersecondact.com

JAM
AT BLUES ON THE RIVER

Have you ever had beer, blues, and barbecue in one setting? If not, you don't know what you are missing! Once a year, the North Shore Riverwalk is crawling with blues fans waiting to get their party on. Blues on the River was the brainchild of Broadway Joe (Joe Booker), Little Rock's legendary DJ. Those who know Joe know that he loves his community. Whether he is coaching a little league football team, raising money for the homeless, or bringing top blues artists to the riverfront, if it has Broadway Joe's name on it, the people will support it! Blues on the River happens in April and has always proven to be a good time. Young and old alike, gather together for a down-home good time!

www.arkansasbluesontheriver.com

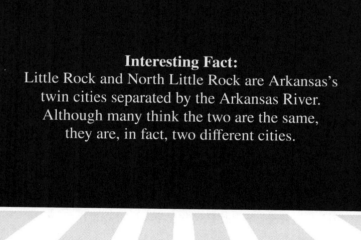

Interesting Fact:
Little Rock and North Little Rock are Arkansas's
twin cities separated by the Arkansas River.
Although many think the two are the same,
they are, in fact, two different cities.

EAT GREEK
AT THE INTERNATIONAL GREEK FOOD FESTIVAL

Okay. I have a confession. I played professional basketball in Greece. After my career was over, I thought I'd have to return to the country to find authentic Greek food. Boy, was I wrong! May 2014, I attended my first International Greek Food Festival in Little Rock at the Annunciation Greek Orthodox Church. Immediately I marked the 2015 date on my calendar. This festival is the largest ethnic festival in Arkansas. Here you can find gyros, souvlaki, and of course, baklava. To go with the traditional Mediterranean cuisine, you can also enjoy authentic music and dance, and even tour the church if you choose. This festival is perfect for family fun. If you decide that you do not want to hang out, don't worry, there is a drive-through line. The International Greek Food Festival is all about the food.

1100 Napa Valley Dr., Little Rock
501-221-5300
www.greekfoodfest.com

Other Food Festivals to Attend

Jewish Food and Cultural Festival
www.jewisharkansas.org/jewish-food-and-cultural-festival

World Cheese Dip Championship
cheesedip.net

The Arkansas Cornbread Festival
www.arkansascornbreadfestival.com

Main Street Food Truck Festival
www.mainstreetfoodtrucks.com

IndiaFest
www.indiafestar.com

LINE DANCE
AT ELECTRIC COWBOY

From salsa dancing to old fashioned boot scoot boogie, you can find it all at Electric Cowboy. A southern favorite with locations in Tennessee, Georgia, Texas, and Arkansas, the Arkansas clubs are the only ones located in the Midwest. Thursday night is Boots and Buckles night, where the fashion is quite impressive. Pull out your favorite pair of boots and your most striking buckle and come enjoy a drink and good ole country line dancing. Wednesday night is salsa night with $3 Coronas and margaritas all night long! If you are not a dancer, join in the Thursday night pool tournament. Remember, you must be twenty-one to enter, doors open at 8 p.m., and the Electric Cowboy has a license to stay open until 5 a.m.!

9515 I-30, Little Rock
501-562-6000
www.electriccowboy.com/littlerock

DIVE IN
AT MIDTOWN BILLIARDS

The folks at Midtown may not know you, but they will treat you like family. A private club that will offer you a membership at the door, make no mistake, Midtown is a dive and a damn good one. This eclectic spot is where you go to play a game of pool or bottle toss and have a cold one. Here you can just be you! However, don't expect linen tablecloths and fancy wine glasses, neither would last a week. Happy hour is 3 p.m.-8 p.m. where they offer fifty cents off all drinks. Midtown is also where you can find the best burger in town after 2 a.m. Their grill is open until 4:30 a.m., and the doors don't close until 5 a.m.

1316 Main St., Little Rock
501-372-9990
www.midtownar.com

TIP
Bottle toss is a big deal here. It happens every Thursday at 7 p.m. Get there early!

CATCH A MOVIE
IN THE PARK

What better way to enjoy a movie than in the beautiful Arkansas weather, cuddled under a blanket with family? As a part of the River Market programming, Movies in the Park is a public event for all to enjoy. The First Security Amphitheater opens an hour before show time, and the movies begin at sundown. If you thought you liked drive-in theaters, you will love watching a film under the stars. The best thing about Movies in the Park is, it's free. According to their website, "The mission of Movies in the Park is help foster a sense of community and enjoyment in downtown Little Rock and throughout Central Arkansas by bringing people together to enjoy a movie in a unique setting along the scenic banks of the Arkansas River." It doesn't get much better than that.

400 E. Markham St., Little Rock
501-375-2552
www.moviesintheparklr.net

Raining? Catch a movie indoors!

Rave Cinemark
18 Colonel Glenn Plaza Dr., Little Rock
501-678-0499
www.cinemark.com

Regal Breckenridge
1200 Breckenridge Dr., Little Rock
501-224-0990
www.regmovies.com

Chenal 9 IMAX
17825 Chenal Pkwy., Little Rock
501-821-2616
www.bbtheatres.com

Riverdale 10 VIP Cinema
2600 Cantrell Rd., Little Rock
501-296-9955
www.riverdale10.com

Regal Breckenridge has reclining seats and Riverdale 10 VIP
serves beer, wine, and a full food menu!

WATCH
A LIVE PERFORMANCE
AT THE ARKANSAS REPERTORY THEATRE

Affectionately known as The Rep, the Arkansas Repertory Theatre has been the backdrop for nonprofit professional theater since 1976. This is not the place to go for the local annual holiday play. The Rep produces high-quality theater with professionals working both behind the scenes and on stage. The productions are more than just entertaining; they are reflections of the highest artistic standards. The Rep is also invested in the next generation through their arts in education programs across Arkansas, where they reach upwards of 12,000 young people each year. Check their website to see what productions the new season will bring. In the past *Les Misérables, Hairspray, Hamlet,* and a host of other classics have been on the bill. Whatever the current season brings, I can guarantee it will be spectacular.

601 Main St., Little Rock
501-378-0405
www.therep.org

PAINT WITH A TWIST
AT PAINTING WITH A TWIST

Sometimes you want something different. Painting with a Twist brings you just that. Whether it's a fun night on the town with friends or a romantic evening, this artistic venue will get your creative juices flowing. The concept began as Corks and Canvas in 2007, but evolved into Painting with a Twist in 2009. Here's how it works: first you visit the website or call to get a schedule of which paintings are being taught on what nights, then you pick a night and make a reservation, and finally you show up with your drink of choice (Painting with a Twist is BYOB) and paint! There are two Little Rock locations, each with different options. If you prefer a private party where you can choose the art you make, Painting with a Twist will accommodate.

400 N. Bowman Rd., Suite 32, Little Rock
501-410-4422

4178 E. McCain Blvd., North Little Rock
501-352-1366

www.paintingwithatwist.com

SING FAVORITE TUNES
AT WILLY D'S PIANO BAR

Who doesn't love a good piano bar? When you combine two musicians going back and forth, there is no way to avoid hearing your favorite tune. We all know once you hear it, you can't help but sing along! Willy D's is very popular, so there is never a dull night. With two full-service bars and a full kitchen, you can eat and drink all you want. They are open 7 p.m.-2 a.m. Tuesday-Thursday. Happy hour is all night on Tuesday and ladies' night is Friday, no cover all night long. Just in case you go on a Friday or Saturday and you want to turn things up a notch, dance venue Club Deep is right downstairs, so you can get your party on!

322 President Clinton Ave., Little Rock
501-244-9550
www.willydspianobar.com

TIP
Pianists not playing your style music? No sweat.
There is another piano bar, Ernie Biggs, right across the street.

SEE AN
OLD SCHOOL CONCERT
AT THE REV ROOM

Great. Live. Music. Period.

300 President Clinton Ave., Little Rock
501-823-0090
www.revroom.com

More kick-ass music spots

Stickyz Rock and Roll Chicken Shack
107 River Market Ave., Little Rock
501-372-7707
www.stickyz.com

Vino's
932 W. Seventh St., Little Rock
501-375-8466
www.vinosbrewpub.com

Discovery Night Club
1021 Jessie Rd., Little Rock
501-664-4784
www.latenightdisco.com

The White Water Tavern
2500 W. Seventh St., Little Rock
501-375-8400
www.whitewatertavern.com

Visit www.arkansaslivemusic.com for a master schedule!

FIND YOUR FAVORITE BEER
AT FLYING SAUCER

You name it, they've got it. With over seventy-five beers on the draft wall and one hundred and fifty in the bottle, Flying Saucer aims to satisfy every taste. Beer snobs love this place. The Little Rock franchise is a large venue with lots of room, so not only can you host a special event, you can sit comfortably and try any beer you'd like. They also have a great menu of bar food and a pool room in the basement. Regular events include trivia night on Tuesday, with two rounds starting at 7:30 p.m. and 10 p.m. Wednesday night is brewery night. If you purchase a specialty beer, you keep the glass. Are you really beer crazy? Join the UFO club and keep track of every beer you drink!

323 President Clinton Ave., Little Rock
501-372-8032
www.beerknurd.com/locations/little-rock-flying-saucer

HAVE A PICNIC
AT MURRAY PARK

When was the last time you had a good old-fashioned picnic? One where you pack lunch and a blanket and sit on the ground? If it wasn't just yesterday, that's too long. Complete with a fishing stream, mountain bike trails, and picnic tables, this is the perfect place to rekindle your love for picnics. Located alongside the river, it has eight pavilions, three soccer fields, a boat dock, and play areas. Locals often use it for family reunions and company picnics. In the warmer months, Murray is a popular place for fishing tournaments. Murray is also pet friendly, offering a fenced, off-leash dog park where our four-legged friends can have fun as well.

5900 Rebsamen Park Rd., Little Rock
501-371-4770

Photos provided courtesy of
the Little Rock Convention & Visitors Bureau.

SIP GRAND HIGH TEA
AT EMPRESS OF LITTLE ROCK

Grand High Tea at the Empress is taken directly from the Victorian era. History tells us that Victorian High Tea was a more formal experience complete with scones and finger sandwiches. There was also a traditional table setting and plenty of rules of etiquette to go around. The Empress has taken a cue from the best. Their Grand High Tea is a replica of history. Tea is served in the formal dining room and everything is handmade on-site. When tea is done, take a tour of one of the most traditional bed and breakfasts in the United States. Remember to call and make a reservation for tea. It only happens on Sundays, and space is limited.

2120 S. Louisiana St., Little Rock
501-347-7966
www.theempress.com

Photos provided courtesy of
the Little Rock Convention & Visitors Bureau.

SPORTS AND RECREATION

WALK, RUN, OR BIKE
ACROSS THE BIG DAM BRIDGE

Little Rock is home to the longest pedestrian and bicycle bridge in North America. It really is a big damn bridge. Ninety feet above the Arkansas River and 4,226 feet long, it's a hot spot for both cyclists and pedestrians. Once you make it to the center, the view is magical. You can use the built-in binoculars to bird-watch, or sit on the bench and soak in nature. The Big Dam Bridge is perfect for exercise enthusiasts. What better way to clear your mind than to jog across the bridge? The lights along the bridge make it a spectacular view from afar. Each year the foundation hosts the Big Dam Bridge 100 Bicycle Tour. To learn more about this event visit www.thebigdambridge100.com.

7700 Rebsamen Park Rd., Little Rock
501-340-6800
www.bigdambridge.com

FIND THE SECRET LIFE OF BEES
AT BEMIS HONEYBEE FARM

This local honeybee supplier does more than just sell everything you will need to become a beekeeper, they allow you to participate in the art. Now before you start running away, thinking of bee stings, hear me out. This place is remarkable. They will be sure you are equipped with protective covering and allow you to interact with the bees as your comfort level permits. You can watch from a distance or get up close and personal. The Bemis family has been Arkansas proud for over thirty years. Aside from the honeybee farm, they also have a pumpkin patch, tree farm, and Christmas tree farm. Call them for more information. What better way to find the secret life of the bees than at a honeybee farm?

13206 Asher Rd., Little Rock
501-897-4931
www.bemishoneybeefarm.com

CHEER
ON THE ARKANSAS TRAVELERS

Minor league baseball is a big deal in Little Rock. Arkansas is a state with no NBA, NFL, or MLB franchises, so we love what we have—collegiate sports and minor league baseball. We take both seriously. Dickey Stephens Park, home to the Travelers, is not your average minor league field. The design is spectacular, without a bad seat in the house. It is also well-kept, and is always nice and clean. In the distance you can see the skyline of the city, which gives it a special appeal. On game day, just like in the majors, there is a lot of fun for the kids and crowd participation. With the beer garden and free Wi-Fi, you can actually attend a game and have a blast without watching baseball at all! Perfect family outing.

400 W. Broadway St., North Little Rock
501-664-1555
www.milb.com

SHOOT HOOPS WITH THE
LITTLE ROCK TROJANS AT UALR

Thanks to Derek Fisher for helping put his college home on the map! The Trojans of the University of Arkansas at Little Rock were once the former NBA standout's team, but now they are Little Rock's team. While the college has a plethora of sports, basketball has become a city favorite. The fifty-six-hundred-seat Jack Stephens Center, where both the men and women play, is perfect for the midsized college. The Trojans compete in the Sun Belt conference, which includes Arkansas State, another Arkansas college located in Jonesboro. Needless to say, this game is always exciting. A Trojans basketball game is the perfect family event. They consistently finish at the top of the conference in both men's and women's basketball, easily making them both exciting to watch.

2801 S. University Ave., Little Rock
501-565-8257
www.LRTrojans.com

CALL THE HOGS
AT WAR MEMORIAL STADIUM

WOOO PIG SOOIE! Go Hogs! Although the University of Arkansas is in the northwest corner of the state, there is plenty of Razorback love in central Arkansas. Playing a 'home' game away from the home stadium can be a challenge, and the U of A is one of very few colleges left that travel to play a home game in their capital city. It's a tradition that is dear to many Arkansans young and old who have witnessed the hogs at War Memorial Stadium. On game day, festivities start early with tailgate parties on the golf course across the street. If you are fancy enough, you can reserve a tailgate spot to be sure you don't miss the party. The best thing about a Hog game at War Memorial is the atmosphere. Since 1948, Arkansans have come together in Little Rock to call the hogs.

1 Stadium Dr., Little Rock
501-663-0775
www.wmstadium.com

For game tickets and dates:
800-982-4647
www.arkansasrazorbacks.com

SLIDE
AT WILD RIVER COUNTRY

It's no secret that summers in Arkansas are hot. Wild River Country is where Arkansans go to cool off! People travel from all over the state to enjoy the water park. The Wave Pool is a longtime favorite for many, but recent expansions have given the park a boost. Wild River Country features twelve rides and has options for all age groups. Smaller children can hang out in the Tad Pool, or drift in the Sidewinder with mom and dad. For those who are a bit more daring, The Thrilling 3 and the Vortex will satisfy your thrill. Anyone can enjoy the good Ole' Swimmin' Hole. Aside from fun, Wild River Country is also affordable. Admission for children two and under is free and they offer military discounts.

6820 Crystal Hill Rd., North Little Rock
501-753-8600
www.wildrivercountry.com

BIKE
THE ARKANSAS RIVER TRAIL

Little Rock has nearly seventeen miles of the Arkansas River Trail that are perfect for biking or running. Outdoor enthusiasts will love the beautiful Arkansas scenery. The trail runs alongside the river and has multiple points of access. There are also bike repair stations, restrooms, and information stops along the trail, making it extremely visitor friendly. The trail welcomes pets as well, but they must be leashed at all times and you must pick up their waste. Just in case you are a horse lover, the Arkansas River Trail features horseback riding trails in Burns Park in North Little Rock and Two Rivers Park in Little Rock.

www.arkansasrivertrail.org

RENT A BIKE
AT BOBBY'S BIKE HIKE

If you like the idea of biking the Arkansas River Trail but don't want to go it alone, stop in at Bobby's Bike Hike. They offer bike rentals and guided tours. You can choose from the Historic Neighborhoods Bicycle Tour, Pork and Bourbon Bicycle Tour, or the Family Edition, to name a few. There are also several types of bicycles to rent, from mountain bikes to road bikes. Rental is available per hour, half day, or full day. You can get a discount if you book online. If you happen to rent a bike you love, check the community bike shop online. Bobby's often sells gently used bikes.

400 Presidential Clinton Ave., Little Rock
501-613-7001
www.bobbysbikehike.com/littlerock

ROLL ON THE RIVER
USING A SEGWAY

Tina Tuner isn't the only one rolling on the river, you can too with Arkansas Segway Tours. A Segway is a two-wheeled self-balancing device (think hover board with handlebars), and a great way to tour the riverfront area or Two Rivers Park. Before you can take off, you must complete a training session. The goal is to be sure everyone is totally comfortable before riding. Although the Segway can only travel about twelve miles per hour, helmets are required. Safety is first! The tour normally lasts about ninety minutes, taking you past Little Rock's best attractions. Tours are narrated by a tour guide, private, and can be customized. When you stop in tell Nez I sent you!

404 E. Third St., Little Rock
501-747-9544
www.arkansassegtours.com

CLIMB
PINNACLE MOUNTAIN

Arkansas is famous for its state parks. If you haven't visited at least one, you are missing out. They don't call it the natural state for nothing! Pinnacle Mountain State Park is located west of Little Rock and was the first near a metropolitan area. While the park features hiking and mountain bike trails, its most popular feature is Pinnacle Mountain. You will find all kinds of people at Pinnacle Mountain. Some run up it to stay in shape, while others hike slowly. With two separate trails, you have your choice of whether to take the East Summit, which is more rugged, or the less rocky West Summit. Whichever you choose, the view from the top will be well worth the hike.

11901 Pinnacle Valley Rd., Little Rock
501-868-5806
www.arkansasstateparks.com/pinnaclemountain

STROLL
THE JUNCTION BRIDGE
PEDESTRIAN WALKWAY

We love our bridges in Little Rock. All of them are well-lit at night, giving the city an ambiance like no other. Aside from how beautiful they look through the windows of downtown hotels, they also can help enhance a romantic evening. After enjoying a meal in the River Market District, you can head to the Junction Bridge Pedestrian Walkway, which extends across the Arkansas River between Little Rock and North Little Rock. Both cities saw the importance of making the bridge user-friendly in 2001, and along with Pulaski County and the Arkansas Highway and Transportation Department, made strides to do so. Today the bridge, complete with elevators and benches, offers pedestrians and bike riders yet another unique way to enjoy Little Rock.

200 Ottenheimer Plaza, Little Rock
501-374-3001
www.pulaskicounty.net/junction-bridge

CREATE YOUR OWN
"WISH YOU WERE HERE" POSTCARD

Once you are done spending time atop the Junction Bridge, take the stairs or elevator down and take a picture through one of Little Rock's human postcard frames. These are life size photo frames that read, "Greetings from Little Rock. Wish you were here!" It's simple: you stand behind one, snap a photo with the landmark in the background, and there you have it, your own picture postcard! Up for a challenge? See if you can find all three! There is one at the Junction Bridge, one under the Interstate 30 bridge overlooking the Presidential Library, and the final one near the Big Dam Bridge. When you snap your photo, don't forget to upload! Use #WishYouWereHere. Contact the Little Rock Convention and Visitors Bureau for more information.

501-376-4781

RUN IN
THE LITTLE ROCK MARATHON

During marathon weekend in Little Rock, everyone is engaged. As a runner, you will not find a city that supports its marathon more than Little Rock. People line the streets, cheering on perfect strangers and offering beverages to the athletes. If you'd like, you can even purchase an Outrageous VIP Experience which will turn the southern hospitality up a notch. The Little Rock Marathon is limited to thirty-three hundred registrants and sells out every year. The Little Rock Marathon is a Boston Qualifier which attracts people from all over the world who flood the streets for a chance to qualify for the big race. Just like any other city, Little Rock offers a half marathon, a 5K run/walk, and a kid's marathon.

500 W. Markham St., Room 109, Little Rock
www.littlerockmarathon.com

GET HIGH
AT ALTITUDE TRAMPOLINE PARK

I don't mean the kind of high that will land you in rehab, but the fun kind that you can only experience at Altitude. Although the company has plans to expand, Little Rock is proud to be among the first ten cities in the world to have an Altitude Trampoline Park. The name says it all. Altitude is a huge open space with trampolines of all kinds where you can dunk like the pros or flip like the Olympians. But be careful, when you come in you have to sign a waiver, so in the event that you don't land your double back handspring like the pros, you pay the hospital bill. To be safe, have fun in the foam pit or play dodgeball. For smaller children, there is a Kids Zone for jumpers under eighty pounds.

15707 Chanel Pkwy., Little Rock
501-353-1281
www.altitudetrampolineparklr.com

SKATE
AT ARKANSAS SKATIUM

Looking for family fun or a unique date? Take a figure skating class at Arkansas Skatium. If you are only in town for a short while, they offer a drop-in session for $12 for the general public; for those who reside in Central Arkansas there is a regular schedule of lessons. If the ice is too cold, slide over to the roller side. Arkansas Skatium has both! In fact, you can pop in and skate on both during public skating times for $10-$20 depending on the package you choose. Because it is also home to the Diamond Edge Figure Skating Club, it hosts competitions from time to time, so be sure to call or check the website before you visit.

1311 Bowman Rd., Little Rock
501-227-4333
www.arkansasskatium.com

PLAY
AT PLAYTIME PIZZA

With a two-story arcade, bumper cars, go-karts, laser tag and mini bowling, how can you not have fun? Playtime Pizza is one-stop-shopping for kids and adults alike. The best thing is, it's all indoors! This means it's open any time of the year. The Pete's Buffet is included in your price of admission and features pasta, pizza, full salad bar, nacho bar, and many other choices. Coke products are unlimited and there is a bar for those twenty-one and over. The facility is available to rent for any kind of group, including corporate parties and team building. They even offer lock-ins and special birthday party packages. Business hours are 11 a.m.-10 p.m. on Fridays and Saturdays, 4 p.m.-9 p.m. Monday through Thursday, and 11 a.m.-9 p.m. on Sundays.

600 Colonel Glenn Plaza Loop, Little Rock
501-227-7529
www.playtimepizza.com

LEARN AND PLAY
AT RIVERFRONT PARK

This is no ordinary public park. Gone are the swings, merry-go-rounds, and sandboxes. They have been replaced with underground tunnels, large climbing stones, a motion-sensor spray pad and yes, even a sculpture garden. This is a park of the twenty-first century. It was designed to inspire imagination and discovery while encouraging innovative thinking. Riverfront Park as a whole features Clinton Presidential Park Bridge, Little Rock Civil War Marker, Riverfront History Pavilion, Junction Bridge, Vogel Schwartz Sculpture Garden, Peabody Splash Park, Medical Mile, William E. "Bill" Clark Wetlands, First Security Amphitheater, Witt Stephens Jr. Central Arkansas Nature Center, and the La Petite Roche Plaza, our city's namesake. The entire park spans eleven blocks along the banks of the Arkansas River. There is something for everyone at Riverfront Park, and the Peabody Splash Park is a great way for the little ones to cool off after enjoying the nature center and our dynamic sculpture garden.

202 La Harpe Blvd., Little Rock
501-375-2552
www.rivermarket.info

DO IT YOURSELF
AT THE PAINTED PIG

What does a young ambitious college grad do when she finds out her neighborhood art studio is closing? She starts her own. That's exactly what Allie Nottingham did in 2007. During her final semester at the University of Central Arkansas, The Painted Pig was born and since then it has kept growing. Today, not only can you make your own pottery, you can purchase pre-painted art-related gifts and design your own jewelry. The Painted Pig is the perfect place to host a group. During girls' night out session, you can even bring in beer and wine. A lot of school-aged artists enjoy hosting birthday parties here as well. Visit their website for pricing and other information.

5622 R St., Little Rock
501-280-0553
www.paintedpigstudio.com

Photos provided courtesy of
the Little Rock Convention & Visitors Bureau.

Just in Case You Love to Golf

War Memorial Park
5110 W. Markham St., Little Rock
501-663-0854
www.littlerock.org/ParksRecreation/golfcourses

Hindman Park
60 Brookview Dr., Little Rock
501-565-6450
www.littlerock.org/ParksRecreation/golfcourses

Rebsamen Golf Course
3400 Rebsamen Park Rd., Little Rock
501-666-7965
www.littlerock.org/ParksRecreation/golfcourses

First Tee of Arkansas
First Tee Way, Little Rock
501-562-4635
www.thefirstteear.org

Big Rock Mini Golf and Fun Park
11411 Baseline Rd., Little Rock
501-455-3750
www.bigrockfunpark.com

Photos provided courtesy of
the Little Rock Convention & Visitors Bureau.

CULTURE AND HISTORY

GET YOUR PASSPORT STAMPED
AT THE WILLIAM J. CLINTON PRESIDENTIAL LIBRARY AND MUSEUM

The Clinton Presidential Library is on the grounds of the William J. Clinton Presidential Center and Park, which also includes the University of Arkansas Clinton School of Public Service and the Little Rock offices of the Clinton Foundation. At the library you can view the complete archives of the Clinton presidency through permanent exhibits together with an exact replica of the Oval Office and the Cabinet Room as well as temporary exhibits that call the center home for a brief time. When you are done witnessing history, have lunch at Forty Two, the full-service restaurant on-site, or catch a lecture at the School of Public Service featuring world-renowned leaders and relevant topics. The center also has plenty of event space for private dinners, receptions, or educational lectures.

1200 President Clinton Ave., Little Rock
501-374-4242
www.clintonpresidentialcenter.org

TIP
Find out more about Little Rock's history through the audio tours.

CONDUCT AN EXPERIMENT
AT THE MUSEUM OF DISCOVERY

Children and adults can find their inner scientist at the Museum of Discovery. With over ninety hands-on experiments, Little Rock's oldest museum brings science, math, and technology to life. Crowd favorites include Tornado Alley Theater and the bed of nails. Most recently, the Museum of Discovery acquired the Guinness World Record musical Tesla coil that produces two hundred thousand volts of electricity. If you are a fan of Jimmy Fallon, you may have seen scientist Kevin Delaney conduct some on-air experiments. Kevin made his way to New York directly from the Museum of Discovery. He had been wowing audiences in Little Rock for years, and locals are very proud to see him on NBC.

500 President Clinton Ave., Little Rock
501-396-7050
www.museumofdiscovery.org

DISCOVER HISTORY
AT THE LITTLE ROCK
CENTRAL HIGH SCHOOL
NATIONAL HISTORIC SITE

In history books across the world, students read about the 1957 desegregation crisis at Central High School. The story of nine African American students, Ernest Green, Elizabeth Eckford, Jefferson Thomas, Terrence Roberts, Carlotta Walls LaNier, Minniejean Brown, Gloria Ray Karlmark, Thelma Mothershed, and Melba Pattillo Beals, who marched into the then all-white Central High School, made national headlines. The Little Rock Nine, as the group has since been called, became the faces of integration and symbols of progression. The complete archive of their story, including video, narratives, and exhibits, can be found on-site. Many of the civil rights legends still have strong connections to the center. Who knows, maybe you will get to shake hands with one of them? Or better yet, listen to them recount events of 1957 in their own words.

2120 W. Daisy L Gatson Bates Dr., Little Rock
501-374-1957
www.nps.gov/chsc

TIP
Want to go deeper? Visit arkansascivilrightsheritage.org/civil-rights-trail for more information on the Arkansas Civil Rights Trail.

After you learn about how it all started, visit Little Rock's Historically Black Colleges and Universities. They are rich with tradition and history.

Philander Smith College
900 W. Daisy L Gatson Bates Dr., Little Rock
501-375-9845
www.philander.edu

Arkansas Baptist College
1621 Dr. Martin Luther King Dr., Little Rock
501-420-1200
www.arkansasbaptist.edu

Shorter College
604 N. Locust St., North Little Rock
501-374-6305
www.shortercollege.edu

EXPLORE A RESTORED ANTEBELLUM HOME
AT HISTORIC ARKANSAS MUSEUM

The history of Little Rock begins here at the Historic Arkansas Museum. The history and culture of Arkansas is celebrated through exhibits, collections, and research. Visitors can explore restored antebellum homes on their original block or learn the history of the Bowie Knife. They can also view collections of art, furniture, pottery, quilts, and jewelry all made by Arkansans. There is also a body of original documents including census records, business ledgers, and newspapers. Historic Arkansas Museum also offers annual family events, day camps, and field trip programs. It's the perfect place to bring school children of all ages, as they have special programming tailored for each grade level. Once you are done learning history here, stop by the Museum of Discovery for a little science. The two are very close to each other.

200 E. Third St., Little Rock
501-324-9351
www.historicarkansas.org

HELP CHANGE THE WORLD
AT HEIFER INTERNATIONAL

It's difficult to describe an organization like Heifer in just a few words. The work that they do worldwide is well-respected and important—and the home office is in Little Rock. A beautiful platinum-green building off Interstate 30, Heifer International is certainly doing its part to make the world a better place. Their mission is simple—to end hunger and poverty—and they are doing so one farm animal at a time. Heifer's systematic model for bringing about the transformation of impoverished economies by giving families farm animals has proven to be effective. The animals not only provide food, but also a way to make an income from the sale of the products they produce. Heifer has a strong presence in Africa, Nepal, Haiti, and throughout the United States, and the vision comes to life right in here in Little Rock.

1 World Ave., Little Rock
501-907-2697
www.heifer.org

BE INSPIRED
AT THE ARKANSAS LITERARY FESTIVAL

Each year the Central Arkansas Library System celebrates authors, screenwriters, and artists from all over the world. With over eighty presenters in the lineup, there is something for everyone. You can catch a Pulitzer Prize winning poet, notable journalist, or even your favorite sports reporter, up close and personal. Adults don't want to miss Author! Author! the opening reception where you can not only get your book signed, but also snap a selfie. Then you can move about town to the varied panels and sessions and be inspired. There is always a special event for children. Many are held at the Hillary Rodham Clinton Children's Library and feature child stars in the industry or those who are specifically working in the genre.

www.arkansasliteraryfestival.org

BUY A BOOK OR PIECE OF ART
AT PYRAMID ART, BOOKS AND CUSTOM FRAMING AND HEARNE FINE ART

Here's an idea: bring in your old books to donate to the free book display, then buy a new one! Opened in 1988, this institution is known for its African American literature. With many bookstores of its kind closed due to the recession, Pyramid still stands. When you are done browsing the book section, take in the latest art display. Right next door is Hearne Fine Art Gallery which houses some of the most profound exhibitions—art lovers, you will not be disappointed! Owners Archie and Garbo Hearne view their space as more than a place to shop, but also as a source of culture and community enrichment. Their commitment to the preservation and promotion of African American fine art and literature is an experience you don't want to miss!

1001 Wright Ave., Little Rock
501-372-5824
www.pyramidbks.net

MEDITATE
AT THE ARKANSAS HOUSE OF PRAYER

In a world that is constantly moving at a fast pace, experts recommend that we take time to center ourselves. The Arkansas House of Prayer is just the place for this. People who are busy with careers go there during their lunch hour just to refuel. Some parents bring their children in an effort to encourage a healthy prayer life. A joint ministry of St. Margaret's Episcopal Church and the Episcopal Diocese of Arkansas, the Arkansas House of Prayer is located in the woods beside St. Margaret's Episcopal Church. It is open to all people, no matter your religious preference, and is a serene place of beauty. Monday-Thursday, 9 a.m.-3 p.m., patrons can check in at the St. Margaret's church office for access. On Saturday and Sunday, you may go directly to the House of Prayer. For security reasons the House of Prayer is not available after dark.

20900 Chenal Pkwy., Little Rock
501-821-7773
www.arkansashouseofprayer.org

SUBMERGE IN HISTORY
AT THE ARKANSAS INLAND
MARITIME MUSEUM

Veterans of WWII told stories of the USS *Razorback* for years after the war. Those who lived aboard the longest-serving submarine in the world were proud of the five combat patrols and many successes of the submarine and its crew. Now, that very same submarine has found a home in North Little Rock at the Arkansas Inland Maritime Museum. Take a tour or have a sleepover. The submarine has functioning heating and air-conditioning and friendly staff available to help you do it all. Before you go down under, be sure to check out exhibits on the tugboat USS *Hoga* (YT-146), the battleship USS *Arkansas* (BB-33), and many others. The Arkansas Inland Museum is certainly the place to go for a glimpse of US naval history.

120 Riverfront Park Dr., North Little Rock
501-371-8320
www.AIMMuseum.org

CELEBRATE ARKANSAS'S AFRICAN AMERICAN HISTORY
AT MOSAIC TEMPLARS CULTURAL CENTER

The story of African American Arkansans is celebrated at Mosaic Templars Cultural Center. Here you can view permanent exhibits that tell both the past and living history of African Americans in Arkansas from 1870 to present. Learn about post-Civil War life which brought about a boom in black entrepreneurship along West Ninth Street, the story behind the Mosaic Templars of America building and organization, and finally, the living history of the Arkansas Black Hall of Fame. Many well-known temporary exhibits have also made a stop in Little Rock, including Shades of Greatness: Art Inspired by Negro Leagues Baseball, The Fine Art of Jazz, and the Inauguration of Hope, a life size memorial to the historic inauguration of President Barak Obama.

501 W. Ninth St., Little Rock
501-683-3593
www.mosaictemplarscenter.com

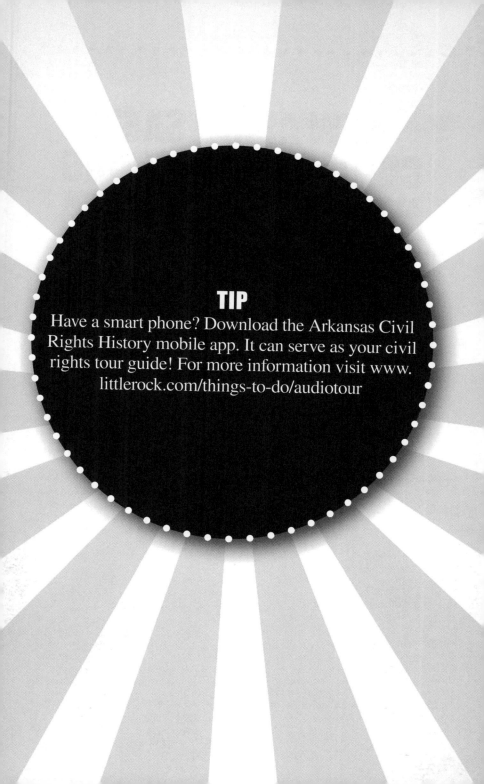

TIP
Have a smart phone? Download the Arkansas Civil Rights History mobile app. It can serve as your civil rights tour guide! For more information visit www. littlerock.com/things-to-do/audiotour

VIEW ARKANSAS'S COLORFUL STATEHOOD
AT THE OLD STATEHOUSE MUSEUM

Another one of Arkansas's National Historic Landmarks, the Old Statehouse Museum is as old as the state itself. Built in 1833, the original building served as the state capitol before becoming a museum in 1947. The museum is home to Arkansas artifacts that help preserve and tell the story of our history. The collections include a quilt exhibit, pottery collection, sports artifacts, Civil War collection, women's history collection, and many more. Two of the most fascinating are the collections of gowns worn by first ladies to government inaugurations and collections from the first families. Here you can find Hillary Clinton's inaugural gown, the typewriter of Governor John Little, and the wallet of Governor Orval Faubus. You can take a guided tour through the museum or go on your own.

300 Markham St., Little Rock
501-324-9685
www.oldstatehouse.com

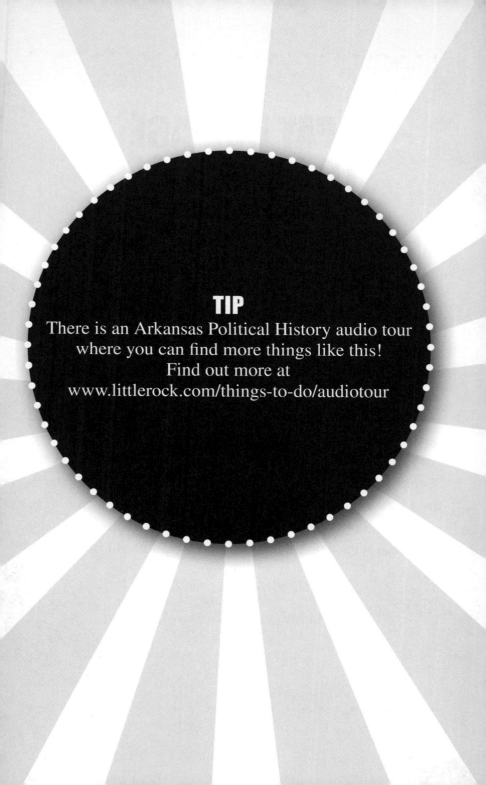

TIP
There is an Arkansas Political History audio tour where you can find more things like this! Find out more at www.littlerock.com/things-to-do/audiotour

PAY HOMAGE TO OUR HEROES
AT MACARTHUR MUSEUM OF ARKANSAS MILITARY HISTORY

Arkansas is working hard to preserve important history for future generations. To learn about General Douglas MacArthur, whose outstanding military career includes a Congressional Medal of Honor, citizens can visit the MacArthur Museum of Arkansas Military History. Located inside a National Historic Landmark, the Arsenal Building, this museum features exhibits dedicated to Arkansas's role in the Civil War. Here you can also find a stained glass window dedicated to David O. Dodd, the Little Rock boy who was hanged as a Confederate spy. Although history of the Confederacy is somewhat controversial in modern day, it still stands as a part of our past. Many lost their lives. You can learn more about their stories and the stories of all of Arkansas's proud military personnel at the MacArthur Museum of Arkansas Military History.

503 E. Ninth St., Little Rock
501-376-4602
littlerock.org/parksrecreation/arkmilitaryheritage

TIP

If this is a family trip, pack a picnic basket. After you enjoy the museum, head over to the playground that is on-site at MacArthur Park. Have lunch by the lake while the children run free.

BECOME AN ART ENTHUSIAST
AT THE ARKANSAS ARTS CENTER

In 1959 what was once just a vision of the members of the Fine Arts Club of Arkansas came to life in a big way. The Arkansas Arts Center was born, adding an educational venue for those who loved the arts or simply wanted to know more. Today, that vision has grown, and so has its influence on the local community. One of the highlights is the Children's Theatre. Here students have a place to perfect their talents outside of school. The Children's Theatre has been recognized as one of the best in the region and performs many of the classics. As another way to show their commitment to the community, the Children's Theatre has "pay what you can" nights. This way no one is denied a chance to experience art.

Ninth and Commerce, Little Rock
501-372-4000
www.arkansasartscenter.org

RELIVE THE GLORY DAYS
AT THE ARKANSAS SPORTS HALL OF FAME

What do Globetrotter great, Reece "Goose" Tatum; famous Oklahoma University coach, Barry Switzer; legendary basketball coach, Nolan Richardson; NBA standout, Scottie Pippen; and owner of the Dallas Cowboys, Jerry Jones, have in common? You guessed it! They have all been inducted into the Arkansas Sports Hall of Fame. There is no question that sports are woven into the fabric of America. Athletic programs have been front and center on civil rights issues and have been successful at bringing people together from all walks of life. The Arkansas Sports Hall of Fame is certainly doing its part to honor pioneers with Arkansas ties who have done their part to add just a small piece to the sports world. Go relive the glory days at the museum; you will be glad you did.

#3 Verizon Arena Way, North Little Rock
501-663-4328
www.arksportshalloffame.com

SEE HISTORY UP CLOSE
AT THE DAISY BATES HOUSE

Daisy Bates was an American civil rights legend. Once the owner of the Arkansas State Press, a statewide newspaper with a focus on African American issues, Bates would go down in history books as the president of the Arkansas chapter of the NAACP who served as the advisor and mentor to the Little Rock Nine. Meetings happened at her home, which still stands today on Little Rock's Westside. It was declared a National Historic Landmark in 2001 and has been restored as closely as possible to her original décor. The most striking thing about the home is the huge bay window. During a time when hate crimes often resulted in bricks being thrown, the window symbolizes Daisy Bates's strength and courage. See history, up close and personal, at the Daisy Bates House. Be sure to call for a private tour. The house is not open to the public.

1207 West Twenty-eighth St., Little Rock
501-374-1957
www.nps.gov/nr/travel/civilrights

REMINISCE
AT THE ESSE PURSE MUSEUM

While many women have a distinct purse collection, there are very few museums dedicated to the handbag. Amsterdam, Seoul, and Little Rock are the only three places in the world with a physical museum. The permanent exhibit traces the evolution of women's purses from the 1900s to the 1990s. Many temporary exhibits including Barbie: The Vintage Years and Handbag for Hillary also travel through. In case you are inspired to pick up something new, Esse also has a store featuring original designs in purses, jewelry, and accessories. Visit their website. Many of the unique designs are available online.

1510 S. Main St., Little Rock
501-916-9022
www.essepursemuseum.com

TAKE A CHILD
TO THE HILLARY RODHAM CLINTON CHILDREN'S LIBRARY

Before she was First Lady of the United States, Hillary Rodham Clinton was Arkansas's First Lady and the Clinton influence on the capital city is evident everywhere you turn. The Clinton Presidential Library helped revive the downtown, and the airport bears both Bill's and Hillary's names, but as a lover of books, I could not be more proud of the Hillary Rodham Clinton Children's Library. Actually it's much more than a library. This is the place where young minds go to grow. They offer many activities and programs for students of all ages. For homework needs, you will find a computer lab and laptops available for check out. Take a child to the children's library where they can witness a building designed just for them.

4800 W. Tenth St., Little Rock
501-978-3870
http://www.cals.lib.ar.us/about/locations/childrens-library.aspx

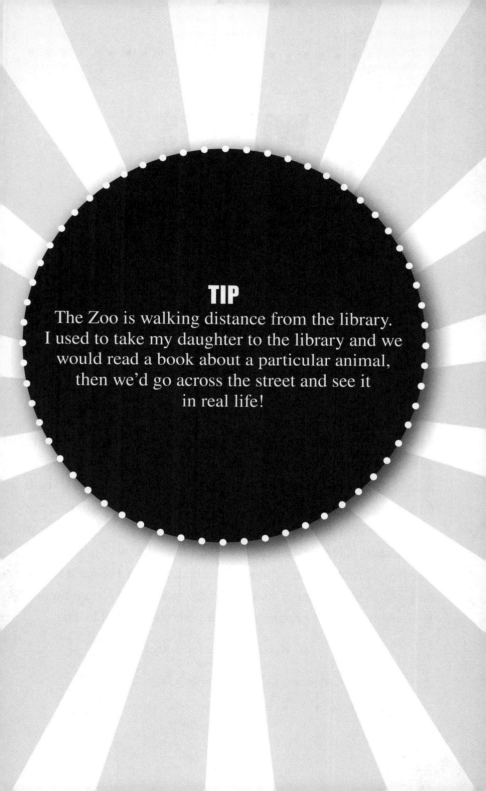

TIP

The Zoo is walking distance from the library.
I used to take my daughter to the library and we
would read a book about a particular animal,
then we'd go across the street and see it
in real life!

WITNESS ARCHITECTURAL EXCELLENCE
AT THE ARKANSAS STATE CAPITOL

Constructed between 1899 and 1915 for $2.3 million, the Arkansas State Capitol is a sight to see. No short description will do it justice. Designed by architects George Mann and Cass Gilbert, the neoclassical style of the building holds true to the twentieth century, featuring six bronze doors and three chandeliers crafted by Tiffany's of New York. Although the building itself is quite impressive, the grounds of the Arkansas State Capitol have several monuments that are certainly worth a visit. You can read the names of fallen soldiers at the Vietnam Veterans Memorial or visit the only civil rights memorial located on any state capitol grounds, Testament, which honors the Little Rock Nine. The Vietnam Veterans Memorial is a smaller version of the memorial in our nation's capital. With over six hundred names inscribed on the black marble wall designed by Stephen Gartmann, the memorial was dedicated in 1987 and is also believed to be the first of its kind on the grounds of a state capitol. Both memorials are popular stops for both visitors and locals.

500 Woodlane Ave., Little Rock
501-682-5080
www.sos.arkansas.gov/stateCapitolInfo/Pages/default.aspx

GO BACK IN TIME
AT THE ARKANSAS KOREAN WAR VETERANS MEMORIAL

Much like the Vietnam Veterans Memorial, Little Rock pays homage to those who lost their lives in the Korean War. Located in the historic MacArthur Park, over four hundred names are listed on black granite panels. The majority of funding for this memorial came from the Republic of Korea, which makes it very unique. Legend says that the country wanted to pay homage to those who helped them gain their freedom. Included in the memorial are seven-foot statues of soldiers and Korean children. This reminds us all of the sacrifice made by military personnel. The Arkansas Korean War Veterans Memorial is said to be one of the most impressive in the United States.

503 E. Ninth St., Little Rock
501-376-4602
www.macarthurparklr.com

LEARN ABOUT TAEKWONDO
AT H.U. LEE INTERNATIONAL GATE AND GARDEN

Little Rock has a unique relationship with taekwondo. Each year thousands flood the streets from all over the world to attend the American Taekwondo Association World Championships. What many do not realize is that the international headquarters for this association is located right here in Little Rock. The H.U. Lee International Gate and Garden honors the founder of ATA, Eternal Grand Master Haeng Ung Lee. Before transitioning in 2000, Grandmaster Lee dedicated his life to sharing the art of taekwondo. The garden pays tribute to his legacy and also serves as a salute to friendship between South Korea and America. The gate which graces the front of the garden was handcrafted by South Korean artisans.

7 Statehouse Plaza, Little Rock
501-376-4781

GET GONE WITH THE WIND
AT THE OLD MILL

In the opening credits of the famous motion picture *Gone with the Wind*, you can see the Old Mill. This landmark located in North Little Rock has been made famous by its appearance in the film and attracts visitors from all over the world. Completed in 1933, the mill was the brainchild of Justin Matthews. Matthews wanted to recreate an old water-powered grist mill from the 1880s for a park area in his new housing development. Today the mill is a city park and the landscaping is cared for by the Master Gardeners of Little Rock. Many use the park as a backdrop for family photos. The Old Mill is said to be the only remaining structure from the classic film.

Fairway Ave. and Lakeshore Dr., North Little Rock
501-791-8537

TOUR OLD VICTORIAN-STYLE HOMES
IN THE QUAPAW QUARTERS

Little Rock has something special for architecture and history lovers alike. Almost ten square miles of restored historic homes make up the Quapaw Quarters. Although Victorian style is my personal favorite, in one block you can view five different types of architecture. The Queen Anne style featuring wraparound porches, classic columns, and huge bay windows is very popular. In an effort to foster appreciation for historic buildings, owners have opened their homes for a spring tour once a year since 1963. Many visitors are so enamored by the district that they decide to become residents. When this happens, they are certainly in good company, as the Arkansas Governor's Mansion is also in the area. The district is managed by the Quapaw Quarter Association. Visit their website for springtime tour dates.

615 E. Capitol Ave., Little Rock
501-371-0075
www.quapaw.com

TIP

Look for The Villa Marre, now a private residence. It was the Sugarbaker Design Studio from the television show *Designing Women*. Also, if you are looking for some fun, try Little Rock's only escape room, both are in the Quapaw Quarters!

Mystery Mansion
2122 S. Broadway, Little Rock
501-580-1325
www.mysterymansionescape.com

RIDE
THE ROCK REGION METRO STREETCAR

Downtown Little Rock and North Little Rock feature replicas of vintage trolleys that give patrons not only a unique way to travel, but also a great way to tour the cities. They connect the twin cities through a 3.4-mile streetcar system that makes it easy to move between attractions. Those being served include the Verizon Arena, the Statehouse Convention Center, and several hotels and restaurants downtown. The drivers give you an overview of attractions as you ride. The best thing about the trolley is that it's inexpensive. With rides costing one dollar each way, it's a fun activity to do with the entire family.

901 N. Maple St., Little Rock
501-375-6717
www.rrmetro.org/services/streetcar

PARTY WITH THE PENGUINS
AT THE LITTLE ROCK ZOO

With over seven hundred animals at the Little Rock Zoo, I find the penguins most impressive. Maybe I'm biased, but there is just something unique about seeing South African penguins in Little Rock. The Penguin Point exhibit opened in March of 2011 and has been a crowd favorite since the beginning. The exhibit boasts a realistic setting for the warmer-climate species of penguins and is the largest the Little Rock Zoo has ever done. Often times you have to drag children away from Penguin Point as they too are fascinated by the animal. The exhibit is also home to many private parties. The Little Rock Zoo offers on-site catering for your special event. Now I'm not saying that the elephants, cheetahs, and reptiles are not interesting to see, but I am saying, don't leave the zoo before you party with the penguins.

#1 Zoo Dr., Little Rock
501-666-2406
www.littlerockzoo.com

TIP
During Halloween Boo-at-the-Zoo is one of the Zoo's most popular events. The adult night is where grownups go to be a kid again.

Photos provided courtesy of
the Little Rock Convention & Visitors Bureau.

SHOPPING AND FASHION

EXPLORE
PARK PLAZA MALL

For a long time, residents of Little Rock went to Park Plaza for all their shopping needs. This midtown mall has been a staple in the community for as long as I can remember. Anchored between the men's and women's divisions of Dillard's department store, here you can find many popular brands such as Abercrombie & Fitch, Banana Republic, Express, and Eddie Bauer. The food court features Chick-fil-A, Moe's, and the local flavor of David's Burgers. Little Rock is home to Dillard's department store's corporate headquarters, so it comes as no surprise that the shopping haven serves as the mall's only major department store; however, Dillard's has it all. From apparel to housewares, this retail giant serves Little Rock well.

6000 W. Markham St., Little Rock
501-661-0053
www.parkplazamall.com

SHOP
AT THE PROMENADE

This outdoor mall in west Little Rock has quickly become very popular. It features thirteen restaurants including Local Lime, BRAVO! Cucina Italiana, and Ya Ya's Euro Bistro. The Promenade is the mall to visit if you want to shop, eat, drink, and see a movie all in the same place. The Chenal 9 IMAX has the city's only IMAX screen running feature films. The Promenade is also where you will find Little Rock's only Apple Store. Enjoy specialty shops like Just Dogs! Gourmet, which specializes in all-natural treats for our four-legged family members; and Belle & Blush, a high-end luxury boutique offering cosmetics, accessories, and a host of other must-haves. Visit the website for a complete directory and be sure to browse Anthropologie; the brand is known for its quality and the store happens to be one of my favorite places to shop.

17711 Chenal Pkwy. #114, Little Rock
501-821-5552
www.chenalshopping.com

FIND A DEAL
AT THE OUTLETS OF LITTLE ROCK

In fall of 2015, three hundred twenty-five thousand square feet of shopping opened in Arkansas's capital city. The Outlets have brought over one thousand jobs to the city and are contributing handsomely to Little Rock's tax collections. Needless to say, so far they have been a welcomed addition. Aside from the retail outlets like Gap, J. Crew, and Old Navy, there is also a Beef Jerky Outlet with more than seventy types of the dried meat, including ostrich. It is not uncommon to find sales promotions at the Outlets of Little Rock; you can view in-store events on the website. Located at Interstates 30 and 430, right next to Bass Pro Shops, you could easily turn this shopping experience into a family affair.

11201 Bass Pro Pkwy., Little Rock
501-455-9100
www.outletsoflittlerock.com

EXPLORE LOCAL BOUTIQUES
IN THE HEIGHTS

Tired of run-of-the-mill shopping? The Heights in Little Rock is the place for you. This charming neighborhood, considered one of the most affluent in Little Rock, offers plenty of upscale retail stores and boutiques. Mostly locally owned and operated, with a few national chains, there is something in The Heights for every shopper. From clothing and accessories to cosmetics and gourmet foods, this eclectic neighborhood is the perfect place for retail therapy. Here you will find Bella Boutique, a fun trendy gift shop; Ember Boutique, which offers creative clothing, art, and jewelry; Terry's Finer Foods, a gourmet food market featuring fresh meat and seafood; and a host of other unique options. Sure, everyone likes a traditional shopping mall, but the shops and boutiques in The Heights offer a shopping experience that is off the beaten path. For a list of stores and shops, visit The Heights Neighborhood Association webpage.

www.intheheightslr.com

TIP
The Heights also offers a great selection of restaurants. ZAZA's and Cafe Prego, which are both mentioned in this book, are in The Heights.

SHOP AND SIP
IN HILLCREST

Although the two are very close, Hillcrest and The Heights are two different neighborhoods. Hillcrest is a National Register of Historic Places location because it is one of the oldest residential districts in the city. Many of the locations mentioned in this book, including Bossa Nova, Ciao Baci, and Kemuri are in Hillcrest. The first Thursday of every month, shops and restaurants offer discounts, later hours, and live music. There is lots of sidewalk traffic during Sip and Shop, some for the drinks, but mostly for the shops. In Hillcrest you can find Hillcrest Designer Jewelry, an upscale diamond whole seller, and HausWerk, a colorful shopping boutique. For a list of merchants, visit the Hillcrest Merchants Association page. You will be glad you did!

www.hillcrestmerchants.net

PICK UP A SOUVENIR
AT SHOP THE ROCK

You can't leave the city without an official Little Rock souvenir. If you are a local who wants to show your Little Rock pride or a visitor who wants to take home a piece of the magic, Shop the Rock is the place for you. They have apparel, books, locally-labeled items, and glassware. You can even find Wicked Mix, Arkansas's own trail mix that will have you salivating for more! Trust me, try the Wicked Mix White Chocolate. It is a winning combination of original, smoky chipotle, and white chocolate. It will make you cheat on any diet! Just in case you have willpower that I don't, Shop the Rock also carries Nettie Joe's Granola, which is also locally-labeled right here in Arkansas.

400 President Clinton Ave., Little Rock
501-320-3515
www.shoptherock.biz

BE NATURAL
AT THE FARMERS' MARKET

Each May through October the Little Rock Farmers' Market is open in downtown. Since 1974, the market, like those in many other cities, has been the go-to venue for fresh fruits and vegetables. But, why stop there? The Farmers' Market in Little Rock features a wide variety of vendors. From locally-prepared foods to arts and crafts, it has become a popular Saturday and Tuesday stop for many. Another unique thing about the Farmers' Market in Little Rock, is that rain or shine, the show goes on! Because it is held in open air pavilions, you don't have to worry about getting wet. For a full list of vendors visit the website below.

400 President Clinton Ave., Little Rock
501-375-2552
www.rivermarket.info/learn-more/farmers-market.aspx

PURCHASE
A TOP-OF-THE-LINE
BICYCLE
AT ORBEA BIKE SHOP

What began as a handgun venture in the city of Eibar in Spain between three brothers evolved into upscale bicycles by 1930. Thanks to Tour De France champion Mariano Cañardo, Orbea gained recognition as a cycling brand. By 1980 the brand was prevalent on the competitive cycling scene and toward the end of the decade had ventured into mountain bikes. Today Little Rock is home to the Spanish bicycle manufacturer's North American headquarters. The Main Street location is a retail showroom for the company's products and features a coffee and smoothie bar. If you are looking for a top-of-the-line bicycle or just want to explore what Orbea has to offer, stop in for coffee and check out a bike while you are there.

700 W. Broadway, North Little Rock
501-280-9700
www.orbea.com

Photos provided courtesy of
the Little Rock Convention & Visitors Bureau.

SUGGESTED
ITINERARIES

PROGRESSIVE DINNER PARTY

A ROMANTIC WEEKEND

WHERE THE SPORTS PEOPLE GO

Cheer on the Arkansas Travelers, 68

Find Your Favorite Beer at Flying Saucer, 60

Shoot Hoops with the Little Rock Trojans at UALR, 69

Call the Hogs at War Memorial Stadium, 70

Find a Deal at the Outlets of Little Rock, 122

FOR THE OUTDOORS TYPE

Walk, Run, or Bike Across the Big Dam Bridge, 66

Bike the Arkansas River Trail, 72

Climb Pinnacle Mountain, 75

Purchase a Top-of-the-Line Bicycle at Orbea Bike Shop, 127

Be Natural at the Farmers' Market, 126

Run in the Little Rock Marathon, 78

CIVIL RIGHTS TOUR

FAMILY FUN

ACTIVITIES
BY SEASON

WINTER

Get Comfortable at Crush Wine Bar, 29

Meditate at the Arkansas House of Prayer, 96

Shoot Hoops with the Little Rock Trojans at UALR, 69

Paint with a Twist at Painting with a Twist, 57

Do It Yourself at The Painted Pig, 83

Explore Park Plaza Mall, 120

SPRING

Catch a Performance at the Robinson Performance Hall, 47

Eat Greek at the International Greek Food Festival, 50

Catch a Movie in the Park, 54

Cheer on the Arkansas Travelers, 68

Climb Pinnacle Mountain, 75

Get Gone with the Wind at the Old Mill, 113

Ride the Rock Region METRO Streetcar, 116

Shop and Sip in Hillcrest, 124

Tour Old Victorian-Style Homes in the Quapaw Quarters, 114

Jam at Blues on the River, 48

Be Inspired at the Arkansas Literary Festival, 94

Run in the Little Rock Marathon, 78

SUMMER

Enjoy Saturday Brunch at Red Door, 34

Cool Off at Le Pops, 35

Get Festive at Riverfest, 44

Learn and Play at Riverfront Park, 82

Party with the Penguins at the Little Rock Zoo, 117

Be Natural at the Farmers' Market, 126

Slide at Wild River Country, 71

FALL

Watch a Live Performance at the Arkansas Repertory Theatre, 56

Walk, Run, or Bike Across the Big Dam Bridge, 66

Bike the Arkansas River Trail, 72

Stroll the Junction Bridge Pedestrian Walkway, 76

Call the Hogs at War Memorial Stadium, 70

Spend a Day at the Arkansas State Fair, 45

INDEX

LITTLE ROCK LOOP

CENTRAL ARKANSAS TRANSIT

408